Depression Cure

Overcome Depression with Feel Good Mood Therapy

Charles Lamont

Table of Contents

Introduction

Everyone suffers from *the blues* from time to time. These are associated with the normal ups and downs of life, and this is mostly natural. However, when the emptiness and the sadness consume you in such a way that it impacts every aspect of your life, then you might have a real problem.

Despair is a natural part of life, in certain situations. You are allowed to feel this way when you have lost a loved one, or when you have just been diagnosed with a serious illness. You are allowed to feel despair when you have lost your job, or if you have just received an eviction notice on your apartment.

Depression is a serious condition. It makes it tough to function, and your enjoyment of life diminishes to the point where you do not have fun doing the things that you used to enjoy doing. Getting through the day becomes overwhelming, and you feel hopeless, as though nothing will get any better.

Understanding depression is the first step to cure. It can be cured, thankfully, but you need to be aware of this monster that is threatening to strip you of your joy.

You need to know the signs and symptoms of depression, and also what causes it. Then you need to be aware of the possible treatments out there, and which one works best for you.

This is the first step to overcoming the problem. And this is what you will benefit from this book. You will be guided through the causes signs, symptoms and treatments of depression. Then you will be introduced to *feel good mood therapy*, and you will see why this is possibly one of the best ways of overcoming depression around today.

Let us first come to grips with what depression actually is, and the different types of depression that are out there…

1: Depression Explained

There are normal reactions to life's struggles. Sadness or downswings are both quite normal after you have experienced a setback or disappointment. These feelings are often mistakenly called *'depression'*, and as a result this often goes misdiagnosed.

Depression is a lot more than sadness, though!

It has been described as *'living in a black hole!'* A feeling of *impending doom* in fact is a more accurate way of describing depression. Depressed people hardly ever feel sad, by the way. They are more likely to feel lifeless, apathetic, or empty. Angry men in particular feel angry, restless, and downright aggressive!

Depression differs from normal, everyday sadness. It engulfs your everyday life, interfering with your ability to function. You cannot work or study. You have difficulty sleeping, and you don't find fun in anything, even in the things that you once enjoyed doing.

Unrelenting feelings of hopelessness, helplessness, and worthlessness overpower you. There seems to be no relief in sight, and you basically have no hope that you will ever come out of your current state. *Snapping out of it* is not an option for you, and you just feel like you will not survive this situation, often resorting to self-harm in an attempt to break yourself free from this feeling!

There are a few things that could indicate that you are suffering from depression. You may be officially *clinically depressed* if you identify with several of the following:

- You have difficulty sleeping
- You sleep excessively
- Concentration is difficult, and tasks that you previously found easy are now a mission
- You are overcome with feelings of hopelessness
- You feel helpless
- Negative thoughts become uncontrollable
- You suffer from a loss of appetite
- You eat way too much
- You are highly irritable
- You have a short fuse, and your temper is considerably shorter
- You find that you are more aggressive than usual
- Alcohol consumption is increased

- You find that you are engaging in reckless behavior
- Life no longer seems worth living, and you are suddenly consumed with thoughts of ending it

Depression varies from individual to individual. You might suffer from a few of the above, or you may actually suffer from all of them. There are various types of depression too, and these manifest themselves in different ways. Let us now discuss briefly what these types of depression are!

2: Types of Depression

Depression has many faces. It manifests itself differently in men and women, and it also manifests itself differently in youngsters and in the older generation! Recognizing these differences ensures that it is treated correctly.

The Faces of Depression

Men are least likely to admit to being depressed. This is because it is often associated with weakness and excessive emotion. Men are therefore less likely to acknowledge these feelings of hopelessness and self-loathing!

They instead claim to be suffering from fatigue, sleep problems, irritability, as well as a loss of interest in hobbies and in work!

Signs of depression in men include aggression, anger, reckless behavior, violence and substance abuse! While women are twice as likely to suffer from depression as men, particularly older men, they are more likely to kill themselves!

Men need to understand that depression is not a sign of failing masculinity. It affects millions of men from all walks of life, of all ages, and it is a completely treatable condition. It also leads to other healthcare situations, like heart disease.

Because men find it difficult to talk about their feelings, depression often goes untreated, with serious consequences. Men tend to focus on the physical symptoms of depression, such as backache, headaches, lack of sleeping, and sexual problems. This is a serious problem, because *men are four times more likely to take their own lives than women!*

Women are twice as likely to admit to depression! Hormonal factors have a large role to play in this. Women suffer from *premenstrual syndrome or PMS, premenstrual dysphoric disorder or PMDD, postpartum depression,* as well as *premenopausal depression.*

Depression in women manifests itself with incredible feelings of guilt, excessive sleep, overeating and weight gain. Women are more likely than men to suffer from **seasonal affective disorder**!

Depression is very common in women. One in eight women, in fact, is likely to suffer from depression at one point in their lives. Feelings of sadness, guilt, and tiredness might mean that you are suffering from depression. The more you understand about depression though, and its implications on women, the more equipped you will be to treat it. The good news is that it is a completely treatable condition!

The *differences between male and female depression* are stark! Women, for example, tend to feel certain symptoms more often than men. Seasonal affective disorder is also more common in women. This is depression in the winter months due to the lower levels of sunlight.

Women are also more likely to suffer from the symptoms of atypical depression.

Atypical depression manifests itself in excessive sleep, overeating, and weight gain. Feelings of guilt, as well as thyroid problems are more pronounced in women. The differences do not stop there though.

While women tend to blame themselves, men usually find someone else to blame. Women feel anxious and scared, while men on the other hand feel suspicious and guarded. Men create conflicts, while women avoid them at all costs.

Women feel sad, apathetic and worthless, and men feel angry and irritable. Women feel slowed down and nervous, and have trouble setting boundaries, while men are restless, agitated, and have a need to feel like they are in control, no matter the cost.

Women tend to talk about feelings of self-doubt and despair, while men on the other hand, think it is weak to talk about such things. Men self-medicate with TV, sports, alcohol and sex, while women self-medicate with friends and 'love'...

Depression in teens is a little more complicated. While some teens appear to be sad, others really do not. Irritability is in fact a more prevalent symptom than sadness, making it a little difficult to diagnose. Teenagers are, after all, very irritable in general.

Depressed teenagers are grumpy, hostile and short tempered. They also experience unexplained aches and pains too. These are all characteristics that are general to teens and adolescents, so that depression is difficult to diagnose.

Untreated teen depression can lead to a bevy of problems. It leads to problems at school and at home, drug-abuse and self-loathing. It could also lead to irreversible tragedies, like homicidal tendencies and suicide. Teenage depression can be treated though, and that is the good news.

Older adults can suffer from the worst forms of depression. This is because their depression is caused by circumstances that are largely beyond their control. Bereavement is one of the main reasons that lead to depression later in life.

You cannot, try as you might, keep your partner alive forever. Loss of independence, especially due to failing health, is another cause of depression in older people. Those without a strong support system suffer especially.

Depression is not a part of old age, though. But since older people tend to complain about the physical symptoms of depression, it is often unrecognized. Depression in older people manifests itself in a number of ways, and is often associated with poor health, high mortality, and an increased risk of suicide. Diagnosis and treatment are therefore very important.

Postpartum depression is another face of depression that is prevalent in new mothers. *New mothers* are known to suffer from *baby blues*, and this is not to be confused with postpartum depression. Postpartum lasts longer, and it is brought on by hormonal changes that are linked with having a baby. This type of depression usually occurs just after delivery, but any depression that you experience within six months after the birth of your child can be attributed to postpartum.

This is a serious depression, and it could manifest itself in detachment from your child, and in extreme cases, homicidal tendencies towards your child. This depression therefore needs to be diagnosed and treated as soon as it occurs, for the safety of the mother, and the safety of the newborn baby.

These are the faces of depression.

Depression can however take on many shapes and forms. Each type of depression can present itself with unique symptoms, causes and effects. You can manage your depression better when you know the type of depression you suffer from. Below are brief descriptions of the various types of depression, to help you get the most effective treatment!

The Types of Depression

The first kind of depression that warrants discussion is known as *dysthymia*. This is a recurrent, mild depression, also known as chronic, low-grade depression. This is characterized by mild to moderate depression for more days than the days where you experience a normal mood.

While the symptoms might not be as strong as those suffered during major depression, which we will discuss next, they do last for a very long time. Symptoms of dysthymia have been known to last up to two years, in fact.

With the severity of these chronic symptoms, living life to the fullest becomes impossible. You cannot even remember times when you were happy, or felt normal. Some people have even been known to suffer from *double depression*, a condition where you experience major depressive episodes as well as mild depression.

Sufferers of dysthymia can feel like they have always been depressed. They may even start to accept their low mood as normal, as just the way they are. Dysthymia is however very treatable, even if you have experienced they symptoms for years.

Major depression is another type of depression! This is also characterized by the lack of ability to enjoy life. You have no ability to enjoy pleasure either. The symptoms range from modern to severe, and they are constant. Some people will experience just one major depressive episode in their lifetime.

Most commonly though this is a recurring disorder, and you may experience several major depressive episodes in your life. The risk of recurrence can be minimized though, with a number of things that support your mood. We will discuss these methods later in this book.

Manic depression is also known as *bipolar disorder*. It is characterized by cyclic mood changes. Depressive episodes alternate with manic episodes. These episodes include hyperactivity and impulsive behavior. Rapid speech and little to no sleep are also experienced during these episodes. The switch from these extremes is typically gradual, and the manic or depressive episodes can last for several weeks, at least.

The symptoms of depression in persons with bipolar are similar to those experienced during major depression. The treatment for bipolar is extremely different with antidepressants. It makes this condition worse. You therefore need to be very careful with the type of treatment you approach.

Finally, *seasonal affective disorder* is a form of depression experienced in winter mostly. As summer passes, many of us will feel sad. This sadness actually morphs into full-on depression in some people though. *SAD* affects about 1-2% of the world's population, and it mostly affects women and young people.

This disorder seems to be triggered by the limited daylight. It typically happens during the fall or winter, and passes or subsides during spring. It is truly a seasonal disorder.

Doctors suggest exercise to combat SAD, especially outdoor activities during the daylight hours. You can also expose yourself to artificial light which may help. Phototherapy, or light therapy, involves sitting next to a special light source, far more intense than your normal indoor light, for about 30 minutes each morning. Light from phototherapy must enter you from your eyes for it to work. Skin absorption has not been shown to be effective.

Light therapy however, has been known to have some side effects. You should be aware of the following possible problems:

- Since it can result in rashes, you should consult your doctor with any skin problems
- Certain drugs or herbs have the ability to make you light-sensitive
- People who are vulnerable to manic episodes can have these triggered by light therapy
- Mild anxiety
- Headaches
- Jitteriness
- Eyestrain
- Waking up too early, are all possible problems

These are the faces and types of depression. Let us now consider some of the causes of depression that are most prevalent and common today...

3: The Causes of Depression

The treatment for some medical conditions is pretty much straightforward. This is because these conditions stem from specific medical causes. You take insulin if you have diabetes, and in the case of appendicitis, you have surgery. Depression is a little bit more complicated.

Because depression is not just a chemical imbalance in the brain, medication is not the only cure for it. In fact, a combination of factors lead to depression, these include psychological, biological and social factors. Therefore, relationships, coping skills, relationships and genetics all play a part in depression.

Certain *risk factors* predispose you to depression however. These include the following:

- A lack of social support and structure
- Loneliness
- A history of depression in your family
- Stressful life experiences
- Financial strains and stresses
- Marital problems
- Relationship problems
- Childhood trauma and abuse
- Unemployment

- Underemployment
- Alcohol abuse
- Drug abuse
- Health problems
- Chronic pain

Knowing the cause of your depression helps you to decide on the best course of treatment. Understanding the underlying causes of your depression goes a long way to help you overcome the problem.

By way of example, if your depression is caused by the result of not being satisfied with you job, then the cure could lie in you finding a better, more fulfilling career.

Antidepressants will not help you to overcome a dead-end job! If, for example, you experience feelings of sadness or loneliness because you are new to an area, then going out there and making friends will be more useful than therapy.

Depression is really often just remedied by simply changing the situation!

While there is no definitive cause for depression, there are definitely things that are associated with its development. No single event usually results in depression. Rather, it is a combination of recent events, and other long-term personal factors that play a role.

Life events can trigger depression in people already at risk. Abusive relationships, long-term unemployment, long-term isolation, loneliness, and prolonged stress at work are such events that can result in you falling into this trap.

Suddenly losing your job is an example of a recent event that could result in depression. A combination of past bad experiences and *personal factors*, including continued difficulties all come together to create an environment that is conducive with the development of depression.

These *personal factors* are many and varied! A *family history* of depression is one such factor. You may be at genetic risk because depression runs in your family. This does not mean that you will automatically suffer from it if a close family member has depression. The circumstances of your life and other personal factors will likely have an important influence in the development of this illness in your life.

Your personality could predispose you to the illness as well. If you tend towards worry, or if you have a low self-esteem, if you are a perfectionist or have sensitivity to personal criticism, if you are self-critical or negative, then you are likely to suffer from depression!

Having a *serious medical illness* can trigger depression too. It can either cause depression directly, or indirectly, through associated worry and stress. This is especially true if your illness requires long-term management, and especially if you suffer from chronic pain because of your illness. Either way, your illness is compounded by the resultant depression.

Most people with depression have a problem with drugs or alcohol, sometimes both, with over 500 000 Australians suffering from depression and some sort of substance abuse disorder at the same time. Recreational alcohol use, and even recreational drug use from time to time is not necessarily a problem.

Some people can actually handle these situations and live productive lives. Where you have a problem, is when the productivity or enjoyment of your life is hampered by substance abuse.

While depression is not just the result of a chemical imbalance in the brain, *changes in the brain* do have an impact in its development. There is still way too much that we do not know about this area, and research is ongoing.

What we do know is this: There are many causes of depression; genetic vulnerability, severe life stresses, some medications, drugs and alcohol, as well as medical conditions are factors that can lead to the mood regulatory function of your brain becoming faulty.

Most antidepressants work because of their impact on the brain's chemical transmitters. You can also use psychological treatments to help you regulate your moods. Some effective treatments stimulate new nerve growth, particularly in the circuits that regulate your mood.

You need to know this, that everyone is different. And while it is a combination of factors that result in the development of depression, it will be different combinations for different people. Apart from these common triggers for depression, however, grief, trauma, financial trouble or unemployment, there are a few little-known causes that are worthy of consideration.

As mentioned before, *seasonal affective disorder* or SAD is common in winter. It affects about 5% of the American population. It is important to note that about 1% of this 5 experience this in summer. People who have trouble adjusting to the new season may experience this when winter becomes summer.

Your body has a hard time adjusting, and instead of enjoying dawn, you struggle to wake up. This may be partially due to imbalances in the brain's chemistry, specifically in the hormone *melatonin*!

Smoking also has a longstanding relationship with depression. People who are prone to depression are likely to take up the habit. This is probably because of nicotine's effect on neurotransmitter activity, which results in higher levels of serotonin and dopamine. This is not unlike the mechanism of action in antidepressants.

When you experience withdrawal though, you may be prone to mood swings. When you stop smoking, you therefore are more likely to become depressed. Avoiding cigarettes altogether though, could help to restore balance in your brain's chemistry!

Depression is also a symptom of *hypothyroidism.* This is a condition where the thyroid doesn't produce enough of the thyroid hormone. This hormone serves many purposes, with one of its primary functions being to act as a neurotransmitter, regulating the levels of serotonin in the body.

Hypothyroidism is perfectly treatable, with medication. So if you experience a new level of depression symptoms, coupled with cold sensitivity, fatigue and constipation, then you should definitely get your thyroid tested.

Sleep deprivation also leads to an increased risk of depression. A study in 2007 found that healthy people who were deprived of sleep, after viewing upsetting images, had greater brain activity than their well-rested contemporaries.

This reaction is similar to that in people with depression. If you do not get enough sleep, then your brain has little chance to replenish its brain cells. Your brain stops functioning properly, leading to, amongst other things, depression!

Facebook depression is a relatively new phrase, one that was coined by experts in the advent of social networking! Particularly teens and preteens suffer from depression associated with too much time spent on chat sites and on social networking sites. People who are addicted to the internet struggle with real-world human interactions, and may lack companionship. Their view of the world may be unrealistic!

A 2010 study showed that 1.2% of the population aged 16-51 spent far too much time on the internet. This study also showed that these people suffered from moderate to severe depression.

Researchers have noted however, that it is unclear whether overusing the internet leads to depression, or if depressed people tend towards the internet to escape.

The *end of something important* also leads to depression. The end of a huge home renovation, the end of a TV series, or even the end of a movie has been known to trigger depression. A 2009 study found that fans of the movie *Avatar* felt depressed or suicidal simply because they discovered that the fictional world created for the movie was not real. Similar reactions were found in *Harry Potter* fans, when the final installments to the film came out, and ended!

Location also plays a role in depression! Research shows that people who live in urban areas are 39% more likely to suffer from depression and other mood disorders than those living in rural areas. This is because people who live in cities have increased activity in the centers of the brain that regulate stress. Higher levels of stress have been shown to lead to serious psychotic disorders.

The rates of depression vary considerably also from country to state. There are states with higher rates of depression than others, and affluent nations tend to have higher rates than the lower-income nations.

Altitude also plays a role, with the risk of suicide going up with altitude!

People are also often overwhelmed by *choices*. If you pick the first thing that meets your needs, you shouldn't have a problem. However, some people respond to this choice overload by reviewing, often exhaustively, the options available to them, until they find the very best item for their specific needs. This coping mechanism is not only linked to perfectionism, but also to depression.

These are some of the causes of depression. Now that you are aware of the root causes, let us now discuss the **signs and symptoms of depression...**

4: Signs and Symptoms of Depression

In short, a person may be depressed if they feel down or miserable for more than two weeks. There are *three categories* of these signs and symptoms, and if you experience several of these for an extended period, then you may be suffering from depression.

You must note though, that most of us will experience some of these symptoms from time to time, and that certainly doesn't mean that we are depressed. The same is true for depression sufferers, in that they will usually not suffer from all of these symptoms.

Behavior is the first category of symptoms. Some of the signs associated with this category are as follows:

- You do not feel like going out anymore. Isolating yourself becomes your crutch and you just want to be alone
- You get nothing done at work or at school, or you get very little done
- You start to withdraw from your close friends and family
- You become reliant on sedatives and alcohol
- You find no pleasure in things that were previously enjoyable

- You lose your ability to concentrate on anything, even the things that you were previously able to focus on easily

The second category is thoughts and feelings. Some of the thoughts that are common in depressed people are as follows:

- "It is all my fault!"
- "I am a failure!"
- "No good ever comes to me!"
- "I am worthless!"
- "Life is not worth living!"
- "People might be better off without me!"

The feelings that you experience during an episode of depression are:

- Sadness
- Misery
- Disappointment
- Unhappiness
- Indecisiveness
- Frustration
- Irritability
- Guilt
- Feelings of being overwhelmed

- Lack of confidence

The third category is the physical aspect. Physically, you could feel one or more of the following symptoms:

- You could lose significant amounts of weight
- You could gain significant amounts of weight
- You can have headaches
- You could experience muscle pains
- You could have sleep problems
- You could feel sick and rundown
- You could feel like you are tired all the time
- You can have a churning gut

Experiencing several of these signs and symptoms could mean that you have depression. To receive more insight as to whether or not you suffer from this illness, you could ask yourself the following questions. Note that this is not to provide you with a diagnosis. For that, you will need to consult with a professional.

Questions that you could ask yourself are:

- How often do you feel tired for no reason at all?
- How often do you feel nervous?
- How often do you feel worthless?

- How often do you feel sad, almost as though nothing can cheer you up?

- How often do you feel like everything is an effort?

- How often do you feel anxious, as though nothing can calm you down?

- How often do you feel hopeless?

- Do you feel restless and fidgety, and if so, how often?

- How often do you find that you cannot sit still?

- How often do you actually feel depressed?

We have now studied some of the causes of depression, as well as the signs and symptoms associated with this illness. Let us now review a couple of the more popular treatments for depression around today!

5: Medications Popular in the Treatment of Depression

There are a large number of drugs available in the US for the treatment of depression. Some of these are more popular than others, and the most popular are discussed below.

Emsam Transdermal is a common drug used to treat this illness. It also appears on the market as the generic, *Selegiline*. It functions as a monoamine oxidase inhibitor. It restores the balance of some of the naturally occurring substances in your brain, known as neurotransmitters.

This drug improves your mood and your general feelings of well-being. It is not a pill though, but rather a *patch* that you use on the skin.

Prozac is a very popular drug for the treatment of depression. It is available in the generic form, *Fluoxetine HCL*. It is used to treat a number of conditions. From depression to premenstrual syndrome, to panic attacks, obsessive compulsive disorder and bulimia, Prozac is a multipurpose drug that treats all of them. It improves your mood, your energy levels, your appetite and your sleep, decreasing fear and anxiety. It may also help you to resist the urge to perform repetitive tasks.

Aplenzin is a drug commonly used to treat and prevent **Seasonal Affective Disorder or SAD**. This depression occurs at one time of the year, usually winter, and it occurs regularly at the same time. It restores the balance of dopamine and norepinephrine in the brain. It has also been known to treat ADHD and also to help people who have decided that it is time for them to quit smoking. It is also used to treat bipolar disorder, along with other mood stabilizers.

Citalopram is another drug commonly used to treat depression! It is commonly called *Celexa*, and appears on the market as the generic, *Citalopram Hydrobromide*. It is known as a *'selective serotonin reuptake inhibitor.'* It restores the balance of serotonin in the brain.

It is also used to treat other mental disorders, from obsessive-compulsive disorder to panic attacks. The hot flashes that occur during menopause are also treated with this drug. It appears in the form of a solid or a liquid, and may be taken with or without food, as directed by a physician.
Finally, *Vivactil* is used to treat mood disorders including depression. It improves your mood, raises your energy levels, and also improves your general feelings of well-being. Belonging to a class of medicines known as *tricyclic antidepressants*, it

affects the balance of neurotransmitters in the brain.

It is taken orally, usually 1-4 times a day, depending largely on your medical condition or your response to treatment. The side-effects of this drug include dizziness, anxiety, and dry mouth. In order to reap the maximum benefit from this drug, you need to take it regularly, though.

These are all perfectly legal treatments for depression. The side-effects though, are often usually adverse, and can sometimes be worse than even the symptoms of the depression itself. *Feel good mood therapy* is an alternative treatment that is available today, and it has no side-effects at all, at least none that are associated with prescribed drug use.

Just what is ***feel good mood therapy***, though?

6: What is Feel Good Mood Therapy?

Feel Good Mood Therapy is basically a *drug-free treatment* for depression! This treatment also cures the many faces of depression, from anxiety, pessimism, procrastination, to guilt and low self-esteem. It is made up of scientifically proven techniques, techniques that will immediately lift your mood, and lead to the development of a positive outlook on life!

Feel good mood therapy teaches you many valuable skills. You learn how to identify the causes of your bad mood and of your mood swings in general. You will learn how to rid yourself of negative feelings, and how to handle guilt. Handling hostility and criticism are also skills taught in *feel good mood therapy*, and you also learn how to overcome other addictions, like the addiction to love and approval

Other valuable skills that you learn with this therapy are the diffusion of anger, overcoming the need for perfection, and you will beat the urge to do nothing! You also learn how to cope with stress, build your self-esteem, avoid the spiral into deep depression, and learn how to feel good every single day!

Feel good mood therapy was developed because people were no longer satisfied with the conventional *Freudian treatments* for depression. It was concluded by *Dr. Aaron Beck* that there was absolutely no empirical evidence that lent itself towards the success of Freud's psychoanalysis in the treatment of depressed people.

It has long been believed that feelings of depression and anxiety stem from our thoughts and perceptions. In fact, it dates back to the Greek philosopher, Epictetus, who stated that *'people are disturbed not by things, but by the way we think about them!'*

Feel good mood therapy is also known as *cognitive therapy*. It is considered to be one of the best treatments available for depression, and has proven to be as effective as, if not more effective than, prescriptive medications.

Cognitive or feel good mood therapy is remarkably simple, despite its effectiveness. It is based on the simple principle that if you think about something often enough, it becomes truth in our minds. Depressed people experience constant thoughts of negativity. These are often also called *cognitive distortions*, and are often a terrible distortion of the reality of the situation.

For example, the belief that you are a failure at everything is logically a distorted perception of the facts. While you may have failed at some things, on close inspection of the truth of your situation, you will see that you have had many more successes than failures.

People who are depressed though, quickly lose sight of their successes. They tend to focus on the negatives in their lives, and lose touch with the reality of their situation very quickly. In cognitive therapy, you are taught to avoid this kind of illogical thinking.

With *feel good mood therapy*, you learn to reframe your thoughts, in ways that are consistent with your reality. If you start to make powerful, truthful statements, and if you do it on a regular basis, you start to feel much, much better.

This is basically what this therapy is, a shifting of your thoughts, towards the more positive, in order to boost yourself towards feeling better. This is a remarkably simple explanation of it, but the effects and impact of this therapy on your state of depression are as remarkable. Let us now see how you can use this type of therapy to overcome depression, and gain control of your thoughts, your mood, and ultimately, your life…

7: How to use Feel Good Mood Therapy to Overcome Depression

We have gone through an explanation of what depression is. We have explored the causes, signs and symptoms of depression. We have seen what some of the more popular medications are for depression, and we have given a short explanation of what feel good mood therapy is, an alternative treatment for this illness that is really taking the world by storm.

We will now get into the meat of this book, the purpose of its creation, and see exactly *how you can use feel good mood therapy to overcome depression*. We will walk you through the various faces of depression, and how you can use this type of therapy to treat this condition.

You need to know this: ***Depression Can Kill You***! It has been called the common cold of psychiatric issues, due to how widespread it has become. The difference between the common cold and depression are rather grim though. Few people, none in fact, have ever killed themselves because of the common cold!

In recent years, the suicide rate has increased. Particularly disturbing, is the suicide rate among children and adolescents. This spike in suicides has happened in spite of the many antidepressants and tranquilizers that have been dispensed in the same time period.

Depression is, fortunately, not a part of a healthy life. It is an illness, and there is a cure! We are not talking about the billion dollar antidepressant industry either, but rather, simple ways of elevating your mood. Feel good mood therapy is a drug-free approach to depression, one that has been developed as a result of scientific research and testing.

People became dissatisfied with the conventional approach to depression. They found them to be slow and ineffective. This revolutionary approach to depression and other mood disorders was developed as a result. This therapy reduced the symptoms of depression, much more quickly than conventional drug therapy and psychotherapy.

How do you apply these feel good techniques to overcome depression then? Let us now discuss how you can use this mood-modifying technology to deal with depression, eliminating the symptoms of this illness, and encouraging personal growth, minimizing future upsets and helping you to cope much better with depression in the future.

There are *four major benefits* of feel good mood therapy that you should be aware of. These simple, yet effective mood-control techniques improve your life in the following ways:

You will first enjoy *quick relief of symptoms*! You can see relief of the symptoms of mild depression in as little as 12 weeks. This is much shorter that the longer duration of treatment with prescription medication.

Secondly, you will also *understand your moods* better! A clear understanding of why you get moody, as well as what you should do to change your moods are things that you will become aware of. You will be taught what causes these powerful feelings inside you, and you will learn the difference between normal and abnormal emotions. You will also be able to assess and diagnose the severity of these upsets.

Thirdly, you will learn *self-control*! Safe, effective coping strategies will be learned, ways that help you to feel better when you are upset. You will be able to develop a realistic, practical, step-by-step guide to help yourself. You will enjoy better, more voluntary control over your moods.

Finally, you will experience *genuine, long-lasting prevention* of future mood swings, as well as *personal growth!* Simply reassessing your basic values and attitudes, those that lie at the core of your tendency towards depression will be learnt.

You will learn too how to challenge and reevaluate your assumptions of your worth as a human being.

The *first step to cure* is an accurate diagnosis of your depression, however. Well, how do you know if you are suffering from this illness? Answering the following questions with *how often* you experience the scenarios, is the first step:

- *How often* do you feel sad and down in the dumps?

- *How often* do you feel unhappy?

- *How often* do you cry or experience tearfulness?

- *How often* do you feel discouraged?

- *How often* do you feel hopeless?

- *How often* do you experience low-self-esteem?

- *How often* do you feel worthless and inadequate?

- *How often* do you feel guilt and shame?

- *How often* do you criticize yourself or blame yourself?

- *How often* do you experience difficulty making decisions?

- *How often* do you have no interest in friends, family and colleagues?
- *How often* do you feel lonely?
- *How often* do you find that you spend less time with friends and family?
- *How often* do you lack motivation?
- *How often* do you lose interest in work and other activities?
- *How often* do you feel no pleasure in life?
- *How often* do you feel tired?
- *How often* do you have difficulty sleeping or sleep too much?
- *How often* do you experience decreases or increases in appetite?
- *How often* are you not interested in sex?
- *How often* do you worry about your health?
- *How often* do you think of suicide?
- *How often* do you want to end your own life?
- *How often* do you find yourself actually planning ways to harm yourself?

If you answer most of these questions with a definitive *a lot* or *always*, then you seriously have a problem. If you answered most of these questions with a *somewhat* or a *moderately,* you also have a problem, although not as severe.

How do you deal with this problem, *overcoming depression*?

Build Self-Esteem

Depression is often accompanied by feelings of worthlessness. If you suffer from severe depression, then these feelings are also severe. The depressed person's self-image is characterized by feelings of *defeat*, being *defective*, feeling *deserted*, and feelings of *deprivation*!

How do you overcome these feelings of worthlessness?

First, *you need to talk back to this inner critic*, to that voice that tells you that you are worthless, unattractive, unintelligent, and so on. There are three ways to overcome this internal self-critic:

1. You need to recognize these critical thoughts and write them down as they appear in your head

2. You then need to learn why these thoughts are illogical and distorted

3. Finally, practice talking back to this voice, developing a realistic system of self-evaluation

A second method involves *monitoring negative thoughts* using a wrist counter. It is an inexpensive piece of equipment similar to a wrist watch that can be bought at any sports goods store or golf shop. The number changes every time you press the button.

Every time you have a negative thought about yourself, click the button. Be aware of all these thoughts. At the end of the day, make a note of your daily score; write it in your log book.

You will notice that the numbers increase in the beginning. As you get better at identifying critical thoughts, you will notice this spike continuing for several days. Soon enough though, your negative thoughts will reach a plateau. The negative thoughts will stabilize for 7-10 days. Then they will start to go down.

This is a good sign. It means that the number of critical, negative thoughts is going down. It means you are getting better. This approach takes about three weeks.

If you decide to use this method, it should not be seen as a substitute for taking a few minutes a day to write down your negative thoughts. It shouldn't take you longer than ten to fifteen minutes. You cannot negate the importance of this step, because it brings the illogical nature of these thoughts out into the light. The wrist counter technique nips these self-critical thoughts in the bud, in addition to the act of writing these thoughts down.

Learn to cope, instead of moping about the situation! Talk to the people involved, the people that make you feel 'useless' or 'worthless'. Find out what their problems are, what difficulties they are having. This gets you to the root of the real problem, instead of trying to solve issues that you actually know nothing about.

Once you have a definition of the real problem, you are in a better position to work towards an appropriate solution. Break the *real problem* down into simple parts, and then attack these problems systematically. Your feelings of inadequacy will start to wane.

Elevating Your Self-Worth

Another thing that leads to depression and anxiety is the feeling that *your worth is proportional to your achievements* in life. This is a remarkably distorted point of view, one that has its roots in the distortions mentioned earlier. You cannot use secular achievements, or achievements in sports and relationships to determine your value as a human being. You need to accept that you are valuable first, before you even start to count your achievements.

This is hard for some people, and it can really become an overwhelming preoccupation, to gauge yourself against your achievements. This is what leads to depression in some folks, and this is what makes people feel like they are worth less than they actually are.

How can you use feel good mood therapy to elevate your self-worth, then?

First, you need to determine whether the personal value you hold works to your advantage, or to your disadvantage. You need to decide, once and for all, that measuring your worth by your achievements is a flawed way of thinking. This is the first step to changing your views, and your philosophy.

It is okay to feel good about yourself when you achieve something. In fact, equating your self-esteem with your accomplishments has definite advantages. This belief system motivates you to produce, in fact. You may push yourself harder in order to win, and once you win, you might like yourself a little more.

There is a flipside to the coin though. If you believe that worth equals achievement, then you may sacrifice the things that bring you enjoyment in the name of career advancement, perhaps. As you throw yourself into your work more and more, you will start to feel withdrawal. Despair and emptiness are characteristics of this withdrawal. In the absence of your achievements, you will start to feel worthless.

It is therefore definitely not to your advantage to link your self-worth to your work!

A simple technique that you can use to overcome your feelings of worthlessness, is a method known as *"operationalization"*. It is basically where you spell out those qualities that make one person more or less worthy than another. You must be aware that this criticism, the insulting things that you think people say about you or to you *happen in your head*!

You tell yourself that you:

- Lack status
- Lack achievement
- Lack popularity, or
- Lack love

So you are the only person who can end this torment for yourself!

Carry on similar conversations with yourself. Create an imaginary opponent for yourself. This opponent will argue that you are worthless or inferior because of an imperfection or lack. Assertively agree with the little bit of truth in these criticisms but follow this agreement with a question: *How is it that you are worthless?*

Write down the worst insults or criticisms that you can level at yourself. Now, answer these criticisms. It will eventually dawn on you, that while you are not as good as other people at certain things, *you are no less worthy.*

The *path to self-esteem* in the absence of achievement is fourfold. First, you need to acknowledge that human worth doesn't exist! It is abstract. You cannot fail at it, fail to have it, or measure it. Worth is a concept, not a thing! Rid yourself from any claim to worth immediately. Then you will never have to fear being unworthy again.

Secondly, it is irresponsible, if you accept the first step above, to engage with, deal with, or handle your worth. Focus instead on living productively, finding or anticipating problems that you might come up with, today, and finding ways to go about solving them! Approaching life in this way creates meaning, and is useful, as opposed to focusing on your personal worth, which is really pointless!

Thirdly, recognize that the only way to lose your sense of self-worth is to punish and persecute yourself with illogical, unreasonable negative thoughts. Choose to fight these negative thoughts, using rational responses, and work your way to self-esteem. Accept that only distortion can rob you of your self-esteem.

The fourth solution towards self-esteem is to treat yourself as you would a VIP who came to visit you for the day. Imagine the wine you would serve them, and the food. Imagine the attention to detail that you would show in your treatment of this person.

Now, treat yourself that way. You don't have to earn the right to treat yourself this way. It is not based on anything that you did. You can just treat yourself better and better, until treating yourself well becomes second nature!

Another trait that lends itself to depression is *perfectionism.* You try to be perfect, and when you fall short, you feel depressed. The depression might be mild, or severe, depending on your level of perfectionism. How then, do you overcome this trait, and thereby avoid the depression associated with it?

You need to understand one thing: *defeating perfection is really the beginning of joy*! Perfection is extremely attractive, and it has a lure that entices you. You strive for it in every aspect of your life, but you must know one thing, that, try as you might, *you will never attain it*!

While *being average* is a little on the dull side, with connotations of not achieving, and not wanting more for yourself than is acceptable, this is *an absolute illusion*. Nobody is ever really average. In fact, you just need to try and be just average, you will not succeed. This is the foundation of how you can effectively use feel good mood therapy to overcome your need for perfection!

Make a list of all the advantages of being a perfectionist. Now list all the disadvantages. You will soon realize that maintaining or striving to maintain perfection actually does not work to you advantage. You will therefore be much more inclined to give up this pursuit, when you realize that it does not serve you at all!

Next, *test the assumptions* made in the list of advantages and disadvantages that you made in the previous step. You have probably never even questioned your perceived inadequacy, because it has become such an automatic reaction, much like the belief that if you were not perfect, you could not perform effectively, or that without your perfection, you are essentially nothing!

Know this, that you are successful not because of your perfectionism, but in spite of it! Seriously! Try out this experiment if you are still not convinced. Make alterations to your standards, and watch the response of your performance to low, middle and high standards. You will be completely surprised by the results!

You will find that by lowering your standards, not only do you perform better, but you also feel better!

So, choose an activity, just one. Instead of aiming for 100 per cent, try for 80 or even 60. You will find that you enjoy the activity much more. You will also find that you become much more productive. It takes courage to aim for average.

But just try it, and let the results speak for themselves!

Assume now that you have decided to *abandon your perfectionism*, just to test the waters. You may find that you have the lingering notion that perfection is possible, in at least some areas of your life. You may believe that if you just tried hard enough, that you could achieve this perfection, and that amazing things will happen once you have achieved this.

The perfection model does not exist however. There is nothing in this world that is so perfect, it cannot be improved upon. You need to realize this right up front. You need to accept this, and you need to stop trying to fit your life into perfection models that really do not exist at all!

Look around you right now for things that need improving. The color and clarity of your TV, or somebody else's clothing, a flower arrangement, a particular singer's voice are all examples of things that can do with a little tweaking. This will convince you that standards of perfection do not fit reality. So you need to stop setting standards for yourself that it is impossible for you to achieve.

Another way to naturally overcome perfectionism, involves confronting your fears. Fear lurks behind perfectionism, almost always. You are driven by fear, for example, to polish things up to the ultimate. You will need to confront your fears if you are attempting to overcome your perfectionism. The payoff for perfection is that it protects you. It protects you from disapproval, criticism and failure! Once you overcome your need for other people's approval, compliments and validation, you will start to lose the fear that is driving your perfectionism, and you will overcome your urge to be perfect!

Developing a process of orientation is another way to overcome your perfectionism. This is where you focus on the process as opposed to the outcome as your basis for evaluating things. Set process goals for yourself, so that you are in control of these processes, and are almost guaranteed success.

For example, as a student, you could set the following goals:

- Attend lectures
- Pay careful attention in class and take notes
- Ask questions
- Between classes, study the course material for certain periods everyday
- Review your notes every 2 to 3 week

These processes are in your control. Your final grade, however, is out of your control, and could depend on the feelings of your professor on that particular day, how high he sets the curve, or on the behavior and performance of other students.

When applying for a job, the following are some goals that you could set for yourself:
- Dress up confidently

- Have a professionally typed and reviewed resume

- Compliment your prospective employer a few times during the interview

- Express interest in the prospective company and get the interviewer to open up about themselves

- Say something positive when the employer mentions their work

- Disarm the negative comments that come from the employer about you by agreeing with them

Again, you are in control of these processes. Whether or not you get the job, is at the discretion of your prospective employer.

Assuming responsibility for your life is another way to overcome perfectionism! Set strict time limits on your activities for about a week. This will change your perspective on life. You will be able to focus on life, and you will start to enjoy life.

Perfectionists are procrastinators. They put things off, waiting for things to be absolutely perfect, waiting for the planets to align themselves just right so that you are then in a better position to make the first move. You only cause yourself misery by holding on to procrastination and perfectionism.

It is great to be able to make mistakes. Go on and enjoy life, and forget about the notion of being perfect. There is a lot more to life than trying to be perfect all the time, and you will lose most of your depressive tendencies if you just let go of your perfectionism.

Now, let us get to the serious issue of *suicide*! Suicidal tendencies are present in about a third of people suffering from mild depression. Three quarters of people with severe depression express suicidal tendencies. This is a real problem, and one which really needs serious attention.

How then, does *feel good mood therapy* help you to handle these tendencies?

First, know that most people are afraid to talk about suicide. They find it particularly hard to talk about their own tendencies, scared of the disapproval that this might insight. They are even afraid that this disapproval might be all the motivation they need to actually take the final step to self-annihilation!

What does this fear mean? Well, it is a good thing, in a way. It is good because they feel that there is just that one step that might motivate them to kill themselves, meaning that the thought to kill themselves isn't yet a solid plan. No matter how solid this plan may be in your head though, it is a good thing that you inhibit yourself from taking that final step towards sealing this deal!

Talking about it is, however, is one of the best things that you can do. This puts your need or your desire to kill yourself into perspective, and you are then forced to face the fact that your desire is irrational. You will be brought face to face with your suicidal thoughts, and you will be able to make sense of these thoughts, and work through them.

Discussing your thoughts with a professional will give you a sense of relief. You will also have a better chance to diffuse this situation before it gets really bad. You will not have a second chance to make right anything that you feel is wrong with your life, anything that is driving you to kill yourself.

You need to evaluate your thoughts. How seriously do you take your suicidal thoughts? Do you really wish that you were dead? Do you have an active death wish? Is your death wish passive? If you have a passive death wish, then, while you would prefer to be dead, you take no active steps to make this happen!

The dangerous death wish is the active one! Are you seriously considering this, thinking of the actual method you will use? What method of suicide have you decided on? What plans have you made for your suicide? The more thought-through your suicide plan is, the more likely you are to attempt it!

If you have a history of suicide attempts, then you need to seek help immediately! You might view these previous attempts as just warming up, and in your flirt with suicide, you never know which attempt is actually going to work. That is why it is extremely important for you to seek professional help!

You need to use your common sense to evaluate your impulses. You know that you are in a high-risk group if you experience one of the following:

- You are severely depressed and have an augmented sense of hopelessness
- You have attempted suicide before
- You have made solid plans for your suicide and you have prepared for it
- There is nothing holding you back from carrying out this impulse

It is vitally important for you to get professional help if you fall in any of the top categories!

There really is nothing that you can do if you do not do serious introspection at first. This is a vital step towards getting the help that you need. You need to ask yourself hard questions, and chances are you will not be able to ask these questions of yourself. You might need to get a little advice from other people who are willing and able to help you. Then you need to take the help that people are offering you.

Common sense is the very last thing that you think you have when you are thinking of killing yourself. It might even be the only thing that you think you have, with your death, your suicide, seeming to be the most logical step for you to take. You need to make a solid evaluation of your impulses though, and then you need to understand how absolutely illogical suicide is. This knowledge is the basis for your feel good mood therapy approach to suicide.

Suicide really is very illogical!

Suicidal people might feel that they have the right to kill themselves. If you are counseling someone with depression who is threatening to kill themselves, you might think that you don't have the right to prevent them from exercising this freedom of choice!

The real question is though, not whether the depressed person has the right to kill themselves, but rather whether they have a realistic idea of what it actually is that they are thinking of doing! You need to ask yourself, when you are having suicidal thoughts, what your motives are for wanting to kill yourself. You need to isolate the problem in your life that is so great that there can be no possible solution to it!

Asking these questions exposes the illogical thinking lurking behind your suicidal impulses. Thinking realistically about things, you will soon see your sense of hopelessness fading, and the urge to live will start to resurface. You will choose joy rather than death, and you will achieve this very fast.

One of the best ways to use feel good mood therapy, or cognitive therapy is to overcome the urge to kill yourself. You can do this by doing simple *role-playing* exercises. You can get a solid perspective of your situation by taking this step outside of yourself, and leaving your case in the hands of abstract individuals.

Imagine that you are two attorneys. Let one attorney argue the case for your living, while you let the other attorney argue the case of your dying. You will then be able to realistically assess your case for life and death, and you will see how absolutely absurd your desire to end your own life is. This is such a simple technique, and yet it is highly effective. In fact, it can be argued that it is the fact that it is so simple, so straightforward, that makes it so very effective.

It might be difficult at first for you to come to any acceptable reasons as to why you should live. You might be so far gone, so lost in your own despair that you can only think of reasons why ending your life is the only alternative to you that makes sense. But how sensible is it to end your life, when you have so many things to live for.

Think outside of yourself for a moment. Think about the person who will find your body after you have killed yourself. It could be your mother. It could be your partner. It could be your child or your brother or sister. How would you feel if there is even the slightest chance that these people are the ones who find you dead?

You will not have a chance to apologize. Whether or not you leave a note, it will not be the same thing as being able to say that you are sorry in person. You will not be able to explain your actions, and you will also not be able to make peace with any of the people that you are currently fighting with. This is reason enough to rethink your impulses.

Death is selfish. There is nothing noble in throwing yourself on the proverbial sword, and you will gain nothing that is worth anything so that you might feel better about yourself. There is no nobility in the temporary relief provided by suicide. Suicide is a permanent thing. There is just no going back from it.

You will see as your attorneys argue their cases, that there really is nothing that cannot be handled, provided you are alive to handle it. You will see that while you may currently be overwhelmed by the events of your life, these are just events, and events pass. Whether you act on them or you don't, nothing in life is stagnant. And, as cliché as this sounds, *nothing lasts forever*!

The transient nature of life is in fact the essence of it, and the reason why killing yourself is fundamentally flawed. Death is the only permanent state in life, and you need to know this. If you kill yourself today, you cannot come back when the situation that led to your killing yourself has passed.

So, there is the basis of feel good mood therapy, and some tips that you can use to apply it in your life, provided you are depressed. You can even use this advice when you are counseling someone who is going through depression. You just need to go through the steps outlined in this book to help you, and use them as a useful reference for the treatment of depression.

There are many other methods and techniques that you can use with feel good mood therapy, and this book could not contain all of these tips. What you need to know though, is that these steps are incredibly valuable, and they are essential for you if you cannot use the more traditional methods of treatment for depression.

There are other *non-drug treatments for depression* out there, apart from feel good mood therapy. These do not offer you a long term solution to the condition however, and this is the advantage of feel good mood therapy, where you can enjoy the benefits of it over the longer term.

This is the most notable difference between this type of treatment, and other non-drug treatments. The following chapter covers some of these treatments.

You can see from the list that some of them are relatively easy to implement in your life, and you should be doing them any way even if you are not suffering from depression. There are simple things that you can do in your everyday life in fact, that can prevent you from suffering from this illness.

Sleep and exercise are the usual suspects, things that should be a huge part of your daily routine any way. There are other things that you can do to boost your mood, and these are outlined in the following chapter. Going through them, you will see whether these actually benefit you. And chances are you will see these benefits almost immediately.

You must be careful though. There are some episodes of depression that are treatable only with medication or a combination of medication and feel good mood therapy or cognitive therapy.

You should therefore not see the things outlined in the following chapter as alternatives to these treatments. What they are in fact, are supportive actions and therapies, treatments designed or suggested to help you through your depression, while you carry out your prescribed treatment.

There really is no quick fix to depression, especially if you are suffering from severe depression, and you should not try to find these. They are not prescribed as actual treatments for depression, merely suggestions designed to support you in your efforts to overcome depression. So, don't be tempted to use these as solutions for your illness.

However, take a look at the following chapter, and choose the therapies and treatments that work for you. Choose the suggestions that make sense to you, and for you and your lifestyle. Implement them in your routine, and see if they have a positive or negative impact to your mood. Chances are, you will see fundamentally positive changes in your mood, and in your life, and you will be inclined to keep these changes in your life over the long-term!

8: Other Non-Drug Treatments for Depression

There are several other *non-drug* ways that you can treat depression. However, if you are having suicidal thoughts, you should probably seek professional help. If you are having homicidal thoughts, seek professional help. Perhaps consulting a *professional feel good mood therapist!*

You need **to *develop a routine!*** Depression tends to strip away the structure from your life, and moments just melt into each other. Get back on track by setting a gentle yet manageable schedule for yourself and you will soon start to see the order return to your life. You need routine!

Set daily goals for yourself! If you are depressed, you will likely start to feel like you cannot achieve anything. This makes you feel worse about yourself. Start with small goals, like say, doing the dishes daily, and then work yourself up from there.

Set achievable goals, and watch yourself edge your way out of depression as you start to achieve them! As you achieve these smaller goals, and as you start to feel better, then you can set more challenging goals for yourself!

Regular exercise encourages your brain to rewire itself properly! It releases endorphins, and has been shown to have other long-term benefits for the depressed. You don't even need to do much exercise, just walking a couple of times a week will help!

There is no definitive research yet on a diet that beats depression. However, foods that are rich in *omega-3 fatty acids*, and *folic acid*, have been shown to benefit people suffering from depression. If you tend to overeat when you are depressed, getting control of your eating could help you to ease your depression too!

Sleep is important! You might find it difficult to sleep when you are depressed, and lack of sleep aggravates the symptoms of depression. Make a point of sleeping at the same time every night. Get up at the same time as well. Do not take a nap. Remove all distractions from the bedroom, including your laptop and your TV. You will find that in time, your sleep will improve.

Never, ever skip a meal! You need to ensure that your blood sugar levels remain stable, since this will reduce your mood swings. Eating regularly leads to this stability, and it makes sure that you do not experience the highs and lows associated with your diet.

Avoiding caffeine is another way to help control depression. Caffeine has, as a side effect, the reduction of serotonin levels in your body. This is counterproductive if you are already predisposed to depression. You need to avoid it therefore, and if you do need to boost your energy, try an L-Tyrosine supplement.

Because vitamin D boosts your mood, you should *expose yourself to direct sunlight*! You should try to get out into the sunlight for at least 30 minutes a day, and without the benefit of sunlight, since some countries don't have enough sunlight, you might want to invest in a therapeutic light box.

Try **meditation** or **creative visualization**. The effects of meditation on your mood are well-documented. You can benefit from settling your mind. Your mood will be lifted, and you will also enjoy a whole lot of other health benefits.

Your mental health will receive a boost from *exercising authenticity* in other aspects of your life too. People often pretend to be something that they are not. The schoolyard, the bedroom, and the boardroom are all places where we are prone to wear masks. We even wear these masks at church, and then we wonder why we are depressed. Decide for a moment, just to be yourself, and see your mood lift dramatically!

Finally, *talking* is a great way to overcome depression. Talking things out with a therapist, a life coach, or even a trusted friend or family member, expressing how you feel about the things and situations in your life that are making you feel depressed will go a long way in getting to the root of your depression. Get the help you need to work through feelings, and this will make all the difference in the world!

If your depression is mild, then try some of these non-drug based alternative treatments. If your depression is severe however, then we really advise that you seek out professional help. Even if you use feel good mood therapy, in severe cases of depression, we would advise that you use a professional therapist to guide you!

Conclusion

Coming to grips with depression isn't easy. You might miss the signs that you are suffering from this illness, because the signs and symptoms mimic other illnesses. But paying careful attention to these symptoms is critical if you are to make a correct diagnosis of your condition, and you will benefit greatly from the effort you put in.

Treating depression is also a little bit complicated. With the barrage of pills around today, we look at these quick fixes to make us feel better in the interim. However, these can become complicated, with the rate of addiction very high, and therefore leading you to further problems.

Feel good mood therapy is the answer to this.

You have seen the simplicity with which this technique can be applied to your life. You have seen how this method can serve you with the simple raising of your self-esteem, and you have been shown how it can be used to treat you when you are feeling suicidal.

These are two extremes of depression, and feel good mood therapy traverses these extremes with ease. What you need to do though, is commit to this treatment. Like many other medicines, you have got to see it through to the end, until you see results and feel the benefits.

You cannot go wrong if you show this commitment to treatment, and you will soon start to reap the benefits associated with this kind of treatment. There are many variations of feel good mood therapy, and various techniques that you can apply, all leading you to the same goal.

If you try one method of treatment, and it doesn't work for you, then simply move on to the next one. You will soon find your grove, and you will find the type of treatment that fits your personality type, and suits you.

Combination treatments are also possible, combining medication and feel good mood therapy. These combinations should definitely not be handled on your own though, and you should consult with a registered professional before you take this route. Professionals have both the knowledge and the experience to guide you through your treatment.

You might want to read this book again, just to get a better idea on what depression is, and what the signs and symptoms are of depression. You need to get to a point where you have a thorough knowledge of what you are supposed to be looking out for, so that you can identify these early warning signs that you are headed for depression.

Then, if you see yourself tending towards depression, you can start today to apply some of the techniques offered up by *feel good mood therapy,* and you will soon start to feel a whole lot better…

www.ingramcontent.com/pod-product-compliance
Lightning Source LLC
Chambersburg PA
CBHW070814290526
45795CB00002B/715